The Frick Collection

Guide to the Galleries

New York · 1979

Cover illustration: The Frick Collection, Entrance

Published by The Frick Collection, New York 10021
Printed in Switzerland
Library of Congress Catalog Card Number: 78-56628
ISBN: 0-912114-10-X

Table of Contents

Preface

This *Guide to the Galleries* was planned for visitors to the Collection who might want to know more about what they are seeing than the summary information provided by labels. It is the first such room-by-room guide to be published since 1947. Edgar Munhall, Curator, wrote the text, drawing information from the six volumes of *The Frick Collection: An Illustrated Catalogue* issued to date and from authors' manuscripts concerning furniture, seat coverings, and gilt bronzes scheduled for future publication. Joseph Focarino edited the *Guide*.

Photography was by Richard di Liberto and previous staff and outside photographers; the views on pp. 6–7 and p. 127 are by Ezra Stoller. Nathan Garland designed the book, which was printed by Conzett and Huber AG, Zurich. Production costs were paid in part by the Fellows of The Frick Collection.

HCF monogram over main entrance

Explanatory Note

While the works of art in The Frick Collection are usually to be found where listed in this *Guide*, items may occasionally be removed from exhibition or relocated. In the latter case, the discussion of a work encountered somewhere other than that indicated in the text can be found be referring to the Index. Since drawings and prints are displayed in rotating exhibitions, they have not been included in the *Guide*. For detailed information on all the works in The Frick Collection the reader is referred to the appropriate volumes of *The Frick Collection: An Illustrated Catalogue*. For summary discussions of all the paintings, including works that may at times be substituted for those described in these pages, see the *Handbook of Paintings* published in conjunction with this *Guide*.

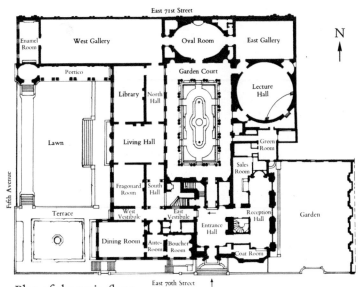

Plan of the main floor

The Frick Collection, Fifth Avenue façade

Historical Note

The Frick Collection was founded by Henry Clay Frick (1849–1919), the Pittsburgh coke and steel industrialist. Upon his death Mr. Frick bequeathed his New York residence and the finest of his works of art to establish a public gallery for the purpose of "encouraging and developing the study of the fine arts." Subsequently a number of additional works, most notably in the areas of painting and sculpture, have been purchased from an endowment left by the founder. This diversified collection, whose historical limits extend from the late thirteenth to the late nineteenth centuries, includes paintings, sculpture, furniture, porcelains, enamels, rugs, and silver, as well as drawings and prints. It is displayed today largely as it was during Mr. Frick's lifetime—without the usual regional and chronological classifications of museum installations. Over the years every effort has been made to preserve the appearance and atmosphere of the original Frick residence, which itself becomes of increasing historical interest, while at the same time all possible use has been made of modern methods of conservation and study.

Mr. Frick grew up in the vicinity of Pittsburgh and throughout later life maintained a residence in that city, as well as a summer house at Pride's Crossing, Massachusetts. From 1905 until 1914 he rented the former Vanderbilt mansion in New York at 640 Fifth Avenue, which contained a large picture gallery, and in 1913–14 he had constructed on the former site of the Lenox Library at Seventieth Street and Fifth Avenue a new residence that is now the permanent home of The Frick Collection. Its architect was Thomas Hastings, and the principal ground-floor interiors were designed by the London firm of White, Allom. The present window hangings and floor coverings in the galleries, with the exception of the Oriental rugs, are copies of those made expressly for the house at that time.

After Mr. Frick's death in 1919 his widow maintained the residence until her own death in 1931. Necessary architectural changes and additions, designed by John Russell Pope, were then made, and the museum opened to the public on December 16, 1935. Constantly increasing attendance over the years required further expansion to meet practical needs, and these were satisfied by the completion of a new wing in 1977. The pavilion was designed by Harry van Dyke, John Barrington Bayley, and G. Frederick Poehler. An adjoining garden was designed by Russell Page.

For a more detailed account of the history of the Collection, consult the essay "Henry Clay Frick, Art Collector," in Volume I of *The Frick Collection: An Illustrated Catalogue*.

Malvina Hoffman, *Henry Clay Frick*

The Entrance Hall replaces the small forecourt and porte-cochère that protected the building's original entrance, which itself has been transformed into the open doorway on the left. In the niche at right is a marble bust of the founder, *Henry Clay Frick,* executed posthumously in 1922 by the American sculptor Malvina Hoffman (1887–1966). The four marble overdoor reliefs represent the arts of Music, Sculpture, Architecture, and Painting.

Reception Hall

Jean-Louis Lemoyne, *Garden Vase*

The first corridor on the right leads to the Reception Hall, the major element of the 1975–77 addition to the Collection building. In a style combining reminiscences of Mansart's Grand Trianon at Versailles and elements of the Italian Baroque, this room provides space for visitors who may be detained from entering the galleries in order to prevent overcrowding. It also gives access to a checkroom at the south end and to the Sales and Information Room at the north. Through the three large windows can be seen the Garden, with its pool and changing seasonal plantings.

In the niche at the north end stands the sole work of art in the Reception Hall—a monumental *Garden Vase* executed by Jean-Louis Lemoyne (1665–1755) in 1727–28 and installed in the garden of the Royal château of La Muette, on the outskirts of Paris. Its attributes of flowers, fruit, and wheat suggest that it may have been intended as an allegory of Summer.

The lower level of the new wing, usually closed to the public, is devoted to a seminar room and a print and drawing room, where the Collection's graphic holdings are stored. Occasionally these areas are used for exhibitions and are then open to visitors. Vitrines in the corridor linking the two rooms display some of the Collection's porcelains.

Piccirilli brothers, *Ceiling Relief*

East Vestibule

Crossing the Entrance Hall the visitor arrives at the East Vestibule, the original entrance to the house. This passage and the elevator lobby on the left are notable for their ceiling reliefs carved in *rosato* marble by the Piccirilli brothers. Hanging on the right is a bronze relief of *The Resurrection* by Lorenzo di Pietro, called Vecchietta (c. 1412–80), signed and dated 1472; it probably once formed part of a tabernacle door. On the marble consoles at the end of the passage are a pair of deep blue covered porcelain jars from the reign of Ch'ien-lung (1736–96) set in French gilt-bronze mounts of an intricate naturalism executed about 1747.

Johannes Vermeer, *Officer and Laughing Girl* (detail)

South Hall and Staircase	The juncture of the East Vestibule and the South Hall provides vistas through the ground-floor galleries north-south from the distant West Gallery to the Boucher Anteroom and east-west from the Garden to the Terrace overlooking Fifth Avenue and Central Park. From the South Hall rises the Staircase leading to the former family rooms on the second floor, now converted into offices. The arched organ screen above the Staircase landing, designed by Eugene W. Mason, takes its inspiration from Luca della Robbia's celebrated *Cantoria* in Florence. It conceals the pipes of an Aeolian organ, the console of which stands in the alcove at the foot of the Staircase.
Paintings	Opposite the organ console hangs the *Mother and Children* by Pierre-Auguste Renoir (1841–1919), painted probably between 1874 and 1876. The identities of the appealing subjects are unknown.

Two of the Collection's three celebrated works by Johannes Vermeer (1632–75) hang in the South Hall—the *Officer and Laughing Girl* and the *Girl Interrupted at Her Music*. The former, painted probably around 1655–60, is a fine example of a characteristic genre scene by Vermeer, representing half-length figures conversing casually in a light-filled interior. The map on the far wall has been identified with one of the Netherlands published in 1621. The girl's headdress, the leaded-glass window, and the chairs with lion's-head finials are similar to those that appear in the slightly later *Girl Interrupted at Her Music*. In the background of the latter work is a representation of Cupid that Vermeer probably intended as an emblem of amorous fidelity.

Between the Vermeers hangs a portrait of *The Comte and Chevalier de Choiseul as Savoyards* by François-Hubert Drouais (1727–75). Dated 1758, the year the artist became a full member of the Academy, it depicts the aristocratic children in the costume of the itinerant workers from Savoy who roamed France doing menial tasks or performing in street fairs, as these two seem prepared to do with their hurdy-gurdy, peep-show box, and trained spaniel. Savoyard children were considered models of filial devotion, which may explain Drouais' choice of disguise.

Farther to the right, over the drop-front secretary, is a portrait of *Madame Boucher* painted in 1743 by her husband, François Boucher (1703–70), in the picturesque disorder of their apartment in the Louvre. The prominent porcelains and screen reflect Boucher's well-known taste for Oriental art objects.

Across the hall is the majestic *Coronation of the Virgin* by

Paolo Veneziano and his son Giovanni (Paolo active 1321–58). It is the last dated work (1358) of Paolo, the leading figure in Venetian fourteenth-century painting. Nearer the Staircase is *The Boatman of Mortefontaine* by Jean-Baptiste-Camille Corot (1796–1875), a dreamy, idealized rendering of a park not far from Paris.

Furniture

On the Staircase landing is a late Louis XIV chest of drawers flanked by a pair of monumental French candelabra of patinated and gilt bronze and lapis lazuli, made about 1785. At the foot of the Staircase rises a tall calendar clock whose elaborate mounts are dated 1767. Its works are by the Swiss-born horologist Ferdinand Berthoud (1727–1807), its case is by Balthazar Lieutaud (d. 1780), who later executed an identical case veneered in ebony for a clock now at Versailles, and its gilt-bronze mounts are signed by Philippe Caffiéri (1714–74). The Frick clock is considered the most important Louis XVI calendar clock to survive and was probably a Royal commission.

Beneath Drouais' *Comte and Chevalier de Choiseul* is a Louis XVI chest of drawers of neoclassical design whose central marquetry panel is signed and dated 1791 at bottom right by its maker, Jean-Henri Riesener (1734–1806). Such a prominent, written signature is rare on French furniture of the period. Like its companion upright secretary standing nearby, the chest was made for Marie-Antoinette, probably for her apartments in the château of Saint-Cloud. The secretary is similarly signed and is dated 1790, but it now seems certain that both these pieces were in fact executed in the 1780s and remodeled, with less elaborate mounts, by Riesener in the early years of the Revolution. Both appear to have been acquired toward the close of the century by the noted collector William Beckford, who owned as well the Frick portrait of *Doge Giovanni Mocenigo* by Gentile Bellini and Claude Lorrain's *Sermon on the Mount* in the East Gallery.

Opposite the secretary is a bench in late Louis XIV style covered with a colorful knotted wool pile fabric depicting flowers, parrots, and squirrels. The fabric was executed at the Savonnerie manufactory between about 1675 and 1725. The French needlepoint covers on the sofa and tall armchairs in the South Hall, along with those on the two matching chairs in the North Hall, form a suite that dates from the late seventeenth or early eighteenth century, with extensive nineteenth-century additions. The frames are modern.

French, c. 1785, *Candelabrum*

Porcelains

The two large Chinese porcelain covered jars with *famille rose* decoration on the Staircase landing date from the Ch'ing dynasty (1644–1912). On the Riesener chest of drawers at the foot of the Staircase is an oval Sèvres jardinière of 1760 painted with birds; a vase of similar form appears in the background of the Frick portrait of the *Comtesse d'Haussonville* by Ingres in the North Hall.

15

Octagon Room

The large doorway at the lower end of the South Hall leads into a small octagonal room that houses two paintings whose subjects are among the most frequently recurrent in Renaissance art—*The Annunciation* by Fra Filippo Lippi (c. 1406–69) and *The Adoration of the Magi* by Lazzaro Bastiani (d. 1512). The former, executed probably around 1440, consists of two separate panels and may originally have composed the wings of an altarpiece. *The Adoration,* done probably about 1475, has a brilliantly ornamented surface belonging to the tradition of late Gothic painting, but it also shows an attention to perspective construction characteristic of the more advanced theories of its century.

The paintings hang over a pair of unusual French consoles in the Turkish style of the late eighteenth century. Made of wood, they simulate the appearance of patinated and gilt bronze with touches of silver. The four small armchairs in the Louis XVI style are covered with tapestry executed at either the Gobelins or the Beauvais manufactory between about 1825 and 1850 after late eighteenth-century designs.

French, late eighteenth century, *Console Table*

Francisco de Goya, *Anglers under a Rock*

Boucher Anteroom

Next is the Boucher Anteroom, where changing exhibitions, frequently of the Collection's drawings and prints, are mounted. This room contains as well the chaste and enigmatic marble *Bust of a Lady* by Francesco Laurana (c. 1430–c. 1502). The two carved and turned walnut armchairs, dating in part from the French Renaissance, are of a type discussed in connection with two similar chairs in the Enamel Room.

The area now occupied by the Boucher Anteroom originally housed a serving pantry for the adjacent Dining Room.

François Boucher, *Painting and Sculpture* (detail)

Boucher Room

Two doorways at left lead into the Boucher Room, where eight panels by François Boucher depicting *The Arts and Sciences* as personified by children have been installed in a setting reminiscent of the mid-eighteenth century. The panels had previously been on the second floor of the building in Mrs. Frick's sitting room.

Paintings

Boucher executed these decorative and amusing canvases of *The Arts and Sciences* around 1750–53 for Madame de Pompadour's château of Crécy, near Chartres. Depictions of the various Arts and Sciences belong to an ancient iconographic tradition, but the present canvases also relate specifically to the personal interests of Boucher's patroness. Beginning at the left of the nearer window, their titles are: *Poetry and Music, Astronomy and Hydraulics* (the boy in *Astronomy* looks through the wrong end of his telescope), *Comedy and Tragedy, Architecture and Chemistry* (the latter with an exploding experiment), *Fishing and Hunting, Fowling and Horticulture, Painting and Sculpture,* and *Singing and Dancing.* The fine blue *camaïeu* landscapes that separate the individual subjects and the panels' splendid floral borders should not be overlooked. The overdoor paintings and reliefs are modern.

Sculpture

The marble bust against the left wall is a nineteenth-century copy of a well-known piece executed about 1750 by François-Jacques-Joseph Saly (1717–76). Many versions of the original exist. It has been persuasively suggested that the subject was the only surviving child of François de Troy, Director of the French Academy in Rome. Boucher seems to have admired the bust greatly, for he frequently introduced representations of it into his paintings, as he did here in *Sculpture,* where it assumes heroic proportions.

Furniture

The Boucher Room contains a choice collection of decorative art objects of the same period and quality as Boucher's panels. In the center of the room, graced with a posthumous portrait of Adelaide Childs Frick by Elizabeth Shoumatoff, is a mahogany writing table with a sliding top, made by Riesener about 1787. Its gilt-bronze mounts display the jewel-like precision characteristic of this cabinetmaker's work.

In the far right corner is a remarkable dressing and work table of about 1772 signed by Martin Carlin (c. 1730–85). Its uppermost section, which is removable and can be used as a bed table, is fitted with a mirror and an adjustable bookrest

Jean-Henri Riesener, *Writing Table* (detail)

19

and has storage compartments probably meant for toilet articles and writing materials. The little table of about 1775 in the far left corner is a typical piece of eighteenth-century functional furniture that can easily be picked up and moved about as needed. Attributed to Godefroy Dester (recorded 1774–90), it is veneered in marquetry that originally was brightly stained in green and yellow.

Against the left wall is a chest of drawers attributed to André-Louis Gilbert (1746–1809) veneered with illusionistic marquetry panels representing floral bouquets flanking a scene of antique ruins complete with white marble sculptures executed in engraved ivory. The seating furniture, lighting fixtures, and woodwork in the room are modern.

**Objects in
Gilt Bronze**

The Louis XVI candlesticks on the Gilbert commode were made perhaps by L.-F. Feuchère (d. 1828) in the late 1790s after a model first executed by Étienne Martincourt about 1775. The andirons, which represent Ganymede and Hebe, cupbearers to the gods, date probably from the first decade of the eighteenth century, when such figural forms for andirons were rare; except for several other castings from the same models, the Frick examples have no close relations.

Porcelains

The porcelains in the Boucher Room are part of a select group in the Collection that were produced by the manufactory located first at Vincennes and then at Sèvres, a favorite enterprise of Madame de Pompadour. In the far right corner, on the Carlin table, is a fan-shaped jardinière dated 1755 decorated by André-Vincent Vielliard (active 1752–90) with a composition after Boucher. On the shelf below it are a water jug and basin of 1776 painted with spectacular arrangements of flowers and fruit by Cyprien-Julien Hirel de Choisy (active 1770–1812). A set of three pot-pourri vases of the type called "*myrte*" because of the myrtle leaves that adorn them stand on the mantelpiece. Jean-Claude Duplessis (d. 1774) probably designed these extraordinary objects around 1760; an unidentified painter decorated them with Flemish peasant scenes after Teniers and landscapes inspired by Boucher. To the left, on the Dester table, is a small four-lobed jardinière of about 1756 painted with birds. Its exquisite form and delicate, spirited decoration are mutually complimentary to an exceptional degree.

Sèvres Manufactory, *Jardinière*

Dining Room

The furniture, chandelier, and woodwork in the Dining Room are modern, designed by the firm of White, Allom in the spirit of English state dining rooms of the eighteenth century. The marble chimneypiece is an authentic work of the period.

Paintings

Except for Gainsborough's dazzling *The Mall in St. James's Park,* all seven paintings here are English portraits of the eighteenth century. The earliest is the one to the left on the south wall representing *Miss Mary Edwards,* painted in 1742 by William Hogarth (1697–1764). The sitter was an heiress who secretly married a spendthrift, Lord Anne Hamilton, but subsequently repudiated the marriage, in effect declaring her child illegitimate, in order to save her fortune. Hogarth's manner was ideally suited to his subject, whose glittering jewels must have delighted his eye as much as her forthright character did his heart. The brilliant scarlet of Miss Edwards' dress is echoed in the nearby portrait by Sir Joshua Reynolds (1723–92) of *General John Burgoyne*, painted probably in 1766, well before Burgoyne's surrender to American forces at Saratoga in 1777.

The three paintings on the opposite wall are all by Thomas Gainsborough (1727–88). That at left depicts *Richard Paul Jodrell*, versatile author, friend of Dr. Johnson, and Member of Parliament. The subtlety of Gainsborough's manner is apparent when this picture is compared with the more robust ones by the artist's contemporaries across the room. *The Mall in St. James's Park*, painted probably in 1783, is a remarkable exercise by a British artist in the genre of the French *fête galante*, a casual gathering of figures in a park. Indeed, in its time *The Mall* was described as being in "the manner of Watteau"— even as "Watteau far outdone." Yet this masterpiece was sold only with difficulty after the artist's death. To the right is the same painter's seductive portrait of *Grace Dalrymple Elliott*, executed about 1782. "Dally the Tall," as she was known, was a great beauty described in her youth as "rosy as Hebe, graceful as Venus." Divorced by her husband in 1776, she had liaisons with various men including both the Duc d'Orléans and the Prince of Wales, who may have commissioned this work.

The portraits at the two ends of the Dining Room are by English painters who lived into the nineteenth century: George Romney (1734–1802) and John Hoppner (1758–1810). The triple portrait of *Henrietta, Countess of Warwick, and Her Children* was, according to Romney's notebooks, painted between 1787 and 1789, though not paid for in full until 1801. Over the mantelpiece at the other end of the room is a double portrait of *The Ladies Sarah and Catherine Bligh* done by Hoppner around 1790. The sketchy landscape at left probably suggests a view of the Thames at Gravesend, as seen from the girls' home.

Sir Joshua Reynolds, *General John Burgoyne* (detail)

Thomas Gainsborough, *The Mall in St. James's Park* (detail)

Silver

The four silver-gilt wine coolers on the south console tables were executed in 1802/04 by William Pitts (recorded 1769–1818), an English silversmith who counted among his clients the Royal family. The arms and crests on the coolers are those of the Earls of Ashburnham. On the west console table stand a pair of silver-gilt coolers dated 1811/12 that bear the mark of Paul Storr (1771–1844), who also executed many Royal commissions. The recurring motifs of the ram's head and the festooned vine leaves and grapes on these objects also adorn the chimneypiece in the Dining Room.

Objects in Gilt Bronze

A pair of deep blue Chinese vases from the reign of Ch'ien-lung, set in superb gilt-bronze mounts of about 1760 attributed to Jean-Claude Duplessis, stand on the mantelpiece. Between them is a mantel clock whose movement was executed by Ferdinand Berthoud, a participant in the creation of the calendar clock at the foot of the Staircase. Made about 1775, this clock is decorated with subjects alluding to love (the sculpted Cupids and billing doves) and time (the star and entwined snakes on the minute hand). Its hour hand in the form of a fleur-de-lis may indicate a Royal provenance.

Porcelains

In the corners at the west end of the room stand two very tall covered vases with *famille rose* decoration dating from the Ch'ing dynasty. On their necks are panels depicting some of the traditional motifs known collectively as the Hundred Antiques. Grouped beneath *The Mall in St. James's Park* are four smaller *famille rose* covered jars from the same dynasty. The naturalism of the landscapes, floral sprays, and birds with which they are painted contrasts with the abstract shapes of the panels containing them, ingeniously imposed on the swelling forms of the jars.

Paul Storr, *Wine Cooler*

Ferdinand Berthoud, *Mantel Clock*

Chinese, eighteenth century, *Ginger Jar*

West Vestibule	This small passageway overlooking the Terrace and Fifth Avenue contains an important group of French paintings and objects of the eighteenth century that serves as an introduction to the adjoining Fragonard Room.
Paintings	The four irregularly shaped paintings by Boucher probably were intended as overdoor decorations; their outlines would have conformed to architectural frames. They represent *The Four Seasons* in a traditional way, but reinterpreted in terms of the pastoral genre still in vogue when they were painted in 1755. Engravings after them by Jean Daullé, dedicated to Madame de Pompadour, bear captions specifying that the originals belonged to the Marquise, but it is not known for which of her numerous residences they were commissioned. On opposite sides of the West Vestibule hang pendant oval paintings representing *Drawing* and *Poetry*. The differences in their quality suggest that the former is by Boucher and the latter by an assistant.
Furniture	The handsome marquetry and ebony desk with gilt-bronze mounts is attributed to the workshop of André-Charles Boulle (1642–1732). It bears the stamp of Étienne Levasseur (1721–98), a Parisian cabinetmaker who probably repaired and restyled this piece originally dating from around 1700. The four armchairs, whose frames may be modern, are covered in unique floral tapestries employing a fashionable motif of bouquets with cast shadows. The tapestries are thought to have been woven at either the Gobelins or the Beauvais manufactory, with each of which Boucher was for a time associated, or possibly in Flanders.
Porcelains	On top of the desk are four blue-and-white Chinese ginger jars with plum-blossom decoration that date from the eighteenth century and curiously echo the outlines of Boucher's *Four Seasons* canvases. Like the other Oriental porcelains exhibited in the galleries, these belong to a type produced largely for export.

Fragonard Room

In the earliest plan of the Frick residence, this room was identified merely as a "salon" and was intended to house, among other things, the suite of furniture with needlepoint coverings now displayed in the North and South Halls. However, when Mr. Frick acquired in 1915 the highly important set of paintings known as *The Progress of Love* from the estate of J. Pierpont Morgan, the disposition of the room was radically altered to accommodate them. White, Allom created a period room in the manner of a sumptuous Parisian interior of the late eighteenth century, employing modern woodwork but incorporating such authentic elements as the chimneypiece, the crystal chandelier, and all the furniture.

Paintings

The history of the series of canvases by Jean-Honoré Fragonard (1732–1806) entitled *The Progress of Love* is complex and incomplete. The four largest panels, on the south and east walls, were executed between 1771 and 1773 for the gaming room of a pavilion at Louveciennes that Madame du Barry, then the mistress of Louis XV, had commissioned from Claude-Nicolas Ledoux. They were installed there for a brief time, but by 1774 they had been returned to the artist as unwanted. The reasons for their rejection are not known, the most likely being that their exuberant style appeared dated within the sober, classical interior of Ledoux's avant-garde building, or possibly that resemblances between their principal figures and the King and Madame du Barry were close enough to be embarrassing. In any case, paintings of a strongly classicizing manner by Joseph-Marie Vien soon replaced them. Fragonard retained his canvases, and in 1790, a year after the outbreak of the Revolution, he transported them, along with his family, to his native Grasse. There, in the salon of a comfortable villa he was sharing with his cousin Alexandre Maubert, he installed the original four canvases and painted ten more—including the two large paintings seen here on the north wall, four overdoors, and four slim panels of *Hollyhocks,* only one of which is now on exhibition. Mounted cheek by jowl in Grasse, the paintings gave the effect of an unbroken panorama, particularly as the windows separating them opened onto a lush Provençal landscape that seemed to continue the garden settings—an effect lost in New York City. The paintings remained at Grasse rather like Sleeping Beauty until the turn of this century.

The four original canvases depict various aspects or stages of love: attempted seduction in *The Pursuit* (south wall left), secret rendezvous in *The Meeting* (right of fireplace), triumphant consummation in *The Lover Crowned* (left of fireplace), and

Jean-Honoré Fragonard, *The Meeting*

tender reminiscences in *Love Letters* (south wall right). Completing the sequence is dejected abandon in *Reverie* (north wall left). The all-powerful force of love surges up from flames in *Love Triumphant* (north wall right)—a panel Fragonard placed strategically in Grasse over a fireplace—and varied moods of love are suggested in the four overdoors: wooing, teasing, anticipating, avenging. As an ensemble, *The Progress of Love* is Fragonard's masterpiece and one of the greatest artistic productions of his century.

Jean-Honoré Fragonard, *Love Letters* (detail)

Jean-Antoine Houdon, *Comtesse du Cayla* (detail)

Clodion, *Satyr with Two Bacchantes*   Clodion, *Zephyrus and Flora*

Sculpture   Standing on the mantelpiece and reflected in the mirror behind
it is a bust of the *Comtesse du Cayla* by Jean-Antoine Houdon
(1741–1828), the only one of the three Houdon masterpieces
in the Collection that Mr. Frick acquired himself. The bust
was exhibited at the Salon in the year it is dated—1777. The
sculptor has presented his subject in the guise of a bacchante
with vine leaves falling across her breast, perhaps in reference
to her husband's family name, Baschi, and to his coat of arms,
which was supported by Bacchus and a bacchante.

Bacchantes reappear in the terracotta group on the commode
at the north end of the Fragonard Room—a *Satyr with Two
Bacchantes,* signed and dated in Rome in 1766 by Claude
Michel, called Clodion (1738–1814). A much later group by
the same artist, *Zephyrus and Flora,* dated 1799, rests on the
commode against the south wall. The evolution of Clodion's
style from rococo to neoclassical is apparent when these two
works are compared.

32

Roger Lacroix and Gilles Joubert, *Commode*

Furniture

No less remarkable than the paintings are the furnishings of the Fragonard Room, a number of which may be of Royal provenance. Certainly so is the massive commode against the south wall. This piece in transitional design bears the stamp of Roger Lacroix (1728–99). It was executed in 1769 for the bedroom of Madame Victoire, daughter of Louis XV, at the château of Compiègne, and records show it was delivered in July of that year by the cabinetmaker and supplier Gilles Joubert (1689–1775). The piece was to be placed beneath a towering mirror of the same width, creating an imposing ensemble. Nineteen years later it stood in Louis XVI's *cabinet de la poudre* in the same château.

Only slightly later in date are the pair of transitional commodes flanking the fireplace which bear the stamp of Pierre Dupré (1732–99), a cabinetmaker by whom few other pieces are known. Their chevron parquetry recalls the flame stitch upholstery fabric popular in the late seventeenth century and transformed in the mid-eighteenth into a geometric veneer pattern for furniture.

Against the north wall stands a D-shaped commode with corner shelves that bears no signature stamp but can nevertheless be attributed to Riesener. Its advanced neoclassical style, severe gilt-bronze mounts, and simple but rich veneer in grained mahogany suggest a date of about 1787–88.

Two similarly shaped side tables *(consoles-dessertes)*, that at right stamped by Riesener, have been placed between the windows; the one at left has only recently been recognized as an extraordinarily good nineteenth-century copy of its mate. Along the same wall are three remarkable small tables: to the right, a three-legged, gilt-bronze table of about 1783 attributed to Martin Carlin, mounted with two exuberantly painted unsigned Sèvres porcelain floral plaques; in the center, an ingenious mechanical work table signed by Carlin and also decorated with plaques of Sèvres porcelain, these bearing the mark of the painter Chauveaux *l'aîné* (active 1753–88) and traceable to the last six months of 1781; and to the left, a gilt-bronze *guéridon* of around 1785 made probably by Pierre Gouthière (1732–1813/14), with classical caryatids supporting a sumptuous plaque of lapis lazuli flecked with gold-colored particles. This unusual use of lapis lazuli in eighteenth-century French furniture recalls the Frick candelabra on the Staircase.

In the center of the Fragonard Room and along the window wall are elements of a suite of sofas and armchairs with frames made about 1760–65 by Nicolas Heurtaut (1720–c. 1771). The tapestry coverings on their backs were woven after figural compositions designed for the Beauvais manufactory by Boucher and first used in 1755; the seat coverings are based on compositions by Oudry and other animal painters. The brilliant and varied coloring of the carved flowers on the frames seems original, but the gilding was redone sometime in the nineteenth century.

The graceful little sewing table with lyre-shaped supports was executed by an unidentified craftsman about 1790, incorporating in its top an unusual Sèvres porcelain plaque made about 1760 and probably cut down subsequently to its present oval shape. Such a table would originally have had a silk bag suspended between the supports beneath its drawer to hold sewing materials. The large, unsigned writing table in Louis XVI style at the center of the room is notable for its elaborate parquetry veneer and gilt-bronze mounts.

Sèvres Manufactory, *Plaque,* from table attributed to Martin Carlin

Pierre Gouthière, attributed to, *Guéridon* (detail)

Executed probably by Quentin-Claude Pitoin after designs by Louis-Simon Boizot, *Andiron* (detail)

Sèvres Manufactory, *Pot-Pourri Vase*

Continuing the pagan imagery of Houdon's bust and Clodion's terracotta groups are the pair of gilt-bronze candelabra with female satyrs displayed on the mantelpiece. Executed probably by the greatest *ciseleur-doreur* of the Louis XVI period, Pierre Gouthière, around 1780, their complex design necessitated casting and assembling over seventy separate elements.

Though slightly enlarged to fit its present location, the Louis XVI chimneypiece in the Fragonard Room closely resembles one made for the Duchesse de Mazarin in 1781, with marble elements designed by François-Joseph Belanger (1744–1818) and bronze caryatid figures executed probably by Pierre Gouthière after models by Jean-Joseph Foucou (1739–1815). Many versions of the original chimneypiece exist, several of them dating from the nineteenth century. The mirror and woodwork above the Frick example are modern.

Like the chimneypiece, the handsome gilt-bronze andirons in the form of flaming incense burners are of a design repeated frequently during the late eighteenth century and into the nineteenth. They relate closely to a pair that were delivered in 1786 to the apartments of Marie-Antoinette and are now in the Louvre. The latter were executed by Quentin-Claude Pitoin (d. after 1786) from models by Louis-Simon Boizot, whose bust of *Peter Adolf Hall* is in the Library.

Porcelains

Four Ch'ing dynasty covered jars with grayish-rose grounds stand on the console tables against the window wall. The similarity of their floral decoration to that on the identically shaped jars in the Dining Room suggests that they were all painted from pattern books.

On the central table is a spectacular Sèvres pot-pourri vase in the shape of a masted ship, one of about a dozen known examples of this type. It forms a set with the two similarly decorated vases dated 1759 on the Dupré commodes. The remarkable birds that ornament all three are probably the work of Jean-Pierre Le Doux (active 1758–61).

On the lower shelves of the mahogany commode against the north wall are a pair of cubical jardinières with Cupids and trophies on a turquoise blue ground that bear the Sèvres date-letter for 1769 and the mark of the painter Charles-Éloi Asselin (active 1765–1804). Their form recalls the wooden tubs used in the eighteenth century to hold orange trees, as can be seen nearby in Fragonard's *The Lover Crowned*.

Living Hall   Because of its central location and the importance of the works of art it contains, the Living Hall is the heart of The Frick Collection. At a glance the visitor can perceive here the eclectic quality of the founder's taste: several masterpieces of European painting, portraits of celebrated historical figures, bronze statuettes by masters of that art, remarkable Boulle furniture, the finest Oriental rug in the Collection, and sumptuous Oriental porcelains.

Paintings   There are only six paintings in the room, but all are of exceptional interest. The earliest and most famous, dating from about 1480, is the *St.Francis in Ecstasy* by Giovanni Bellini (c. 1430–1516). This picture commemorates the moment in the life of St.Francis of Assisi when, during a retreat on Mount Alvernia, he beheld a vision of Christ crucified that left upon his body the marks of Christ's wounds—the Stigmata. Unlike earlier artists Bellini did not depict the vision itself, but instead suggested an awesome power flooding the landscape with a glorious light and bending the tree at left as if before a violent wind.

The portraits to either side are by Titian (1477/90–1576). The contemplative one at left, depicting a young *Man in a Red Cap,* was executed about 1516 during the artist's early career, while he was still under the influence of Giorgione. On the right is Titian's imposing portrait of *Pietro Aretino,* called the "Scourge of Princes"—a notorious author of letters, satires, verses, and comedies.

Aretino's powerful presence contrasts with the gentle hesitancy of the unidentified youth much in the way that—across the room—the forthright image of *Sir Thomas More* by Hans Holbein the Younger (1497/98–1543) contrasts with the same artist's likeness of More's crafty enemy *Thomas Cromwell.* Holbein arrived in England in 1526 and painted More's portrait the following year. More later served as Lord Chancellor to Henry VIII, but after refusing to support Henry's antipapal policies he was convicted of treason and decapitated. Cromwell, a blacksmith's son who rose to the post of Lord Great Chamberlain, was largely responsible for More's execution, but he subsequently lost Royal favor and was himself accused of treason and beheaded.

From its position over the fireplace, the *St. Jerome* painted about 1590–1600 by El Greco (1541–1614) dominates the room. Dressed in the robes of a cardinal, the saint rests his hands on the Vulgate, his Latin translation of the Bible. A number of versions of this painting by El Greco exist.

Titian, *Man in a Red Cap*

Sculpture   Several choice Italian bronze statuettes can be found in the Living Hall, part of a group that Mr. Frick acquired largely from the estate of J. Pierpont Morgan. These include, beneath Titian's *Man in a Red Cap,* one of the masterpieces of Paduan bronze sculpture—the *Neptune on a Sea-Monster* by Severo Calzetta, called Severo da Ravenna (late fifteenth–early sixteenth centuries). Attributed to Severo on the basis of resemblances to his only signed bronze, the Frick group is the

The Living Hall, seen in a recent view (above) and as it appeared in the 1920s (left), before the Collection was opened to the public

Hans Holbein the Younger, *Sir Thomas More* (detail)

finest example of a large number of interrelated sculptures
whose precise iconographical significance is unknown.

Beneath the portrait of *Aretino* is the celebrated *Hercules* by
Antonio Pollajuolo (1426/32–98), one of only three surviving
small bronzes by this Florentine sculptor, painter, and engraver.
Its rough surface, which indicates it was never quite completed,
gives it an extremely bold character, appropriate to the subject.

A much different *Hercules* is that executed by Pier Jacopo
Alari Bonacolsi (c. 1460–1528), displayed across the room
beneath the *Cromwell* portrait. Called Antico because of his
deliberately classicizing style and his connoisseurship of ancient
art, the sculptor created here a work in the manner of a highly
finished Hellenistic bronze, complete to the silvered eyes and
gilded hair and lion's skin.

Under Holbein's *More* is a group of *Virtue Triumphant Over
Vice*, a modified reduction of Giovanni Bologna's famous
large-scale marble of *Florence Triumphant Over Pisa*. Done by
the sculptor Massimiliano Soldani (1658–1740), it is probably
one of a series of reduced copies he made of famous statues in
his native Florence.

On the writing table at the center of the room is a *Marine
Nymph* believed to be an eighteenth-century version of a work
executed by Stoldo Lorenzi (1534–83) for the Studiolo in the
Palazzo Vecchio, Florence. The firedogs with finial figures of
Jupiter and *Venus* are from a Venetian workshop of the late
eighteenth or early nineteenth century; the figures are based
on much earlier models by Alessandro Vittoria (1525–1608).

Antonio Pollajuolo, *Hercules* (detail)

Rug

The large figured rug under the writing table is Persian, attributed to the sixteenth-century looms of Herat. To the Persians the patterns of such great floral rugs represented gardens. The design of this one also incorporates stylized Chinese motifs which are found again on Oriental porcelains in the Collection.

Persian, attributed to Herat,
sixteenth century, *Rug*

Workshop of André-Charles Boulle,
attributed to, *Pedestal*

André-Charles Boulle,
Writing Table (detail)

Furniture	The Living Hall contains seven pieces of furniture by or in the manner of André-Charles Boulle, a cabinetmaker to Louis XIV who specialized in furniture veneered with panels of tortoiseshell and brass framed in ebony and set off by gilt-bronze mounts. Such furniture, while intended to be functional, has come to be regarded more as a sort of decorative sculpture.

The central writing table of about 1710 can be attributed securely to the workshop of the master. Certain of its mounts, however, such as the masks flanking the middle drawer, date from about 1735, indicating that the piece was remodeled at that time to conform to current tastes.

Between the windows on the east wall are a pair of octagonal pedestals made about 1695 and attributed to Boulle's workshop as well. Their form is very rare. Their *première partie* and *contre-partie* marquetry panels demonstrate Boulle's method of cutting out simultaneously two sheets of veneer in different materials and then combining the resulting layers so that one set is the reverse design of the other.

Between the windows on the west wall are two later cabinets imitating the manner of Boulle, that on the left mounted with a medallion representing Henri IV, that on the right bearing a likeness of the King's faithful minister the Duc de Sully. On the south wall, under the Titian portraits, are a pair of nineteenth-century English copies of Boulle's famous "sarcophagus" chests at Versailles.

Somewhat reminiscent of Boulle's sober style are the cabinets with ebony veneer, lacquer panels, and porphyry tops on either side of the fireplace. They were executed about 1765 by one of the members of the Vanrisamburgh family, long known only by the initials with which they stamped their work: BVRB. The high quality of their design, their mounts, and their fine black-and-gold Japanese lacquer panels suggest an attribution to Bernard II Vanrisamburgh (d. before 1767).

The chairs along the east and west walls are in seventeenth-century English style, and the remaining furniture is modern.

Porcelains	The Oriental porcelains in the Living Hall include two large covered jars with *famille rose* decoration on a black ground standing on the pedestals between the east windows, a pair of vases in the form of ancient ceremonial bronzes on the mantelpiece, and a delightful pair of elaborately patterned figures of ladies on stands set on the cabinets between the west windows. All date from the Ch'ing dynasty.

45

Bernard II Vanrisamburgh, attributed to, *Cabinet* (detail)

Chinese, Ch'ing dynasty, *Large Covered Jar with* Famille Rose *Decoration*

Library

While the paintings in this room are nearly all British works of the eighteenth and nineteenth centuries, the objects range from Italian Renaissance bronzes to Chinese porcelains and eighteenth-century French gilt-bronze decorative furnishings. The woodwork (for which the model is preserved in the Museum of the City of New York) is modern; the elaborate carving over the chimneypiece, in the manner of Grinling Gibbons, is by Abraham Miller. The books are modern editions, mostly of literary and historical works.

Paintings

The portrait of the founder of the Collection that hangs over the fireplace is a posthumous one executed in 1943 by the American painter John C. Johansen (1876–1964).

Along the south and east walls to the right of the Living Hall door hangs a remarkable trio of portraits: the dazzling *Julia, Lady Peel,* wife of the eminent statesman Sir Robert Peel, painted by Sir Thomas Lawrence (1769–1830); *George Washington* by Gilbert Stuart (1755–1828), one of the many versions of this image that Stuart was to produce; and the deservedly popular *Lady Hamilton as 'Nature'* by George Romney, painted when this blacksmith's daughter was the mistress of Charles Greville, about a decade before she began her famous liaison

Joseph Mallord William Turner, *Mortlake Terrace: Early Summer Morning*

with Lord Nelson. The allegorical title and conception of the
Lady Hamilton portrait are typical of the many likenesses
Romney painted of her.

To the right of the fireplace is *Mortlake Terrace: Early
Summer Morning* by Joseph Mallord William Turner (1775–1851),
a depiction of a house still standing beside the Thames just
outside London. The picture is an original variation on the
theme of waterscapes painted in earlier centuries by the Dutch
and Venetian painters Turner so admired. To the left of the
fireplace is another water scene by Turner with historical
reminiscences: *Antwerp: Van Goyen Looking Out for a Subject.*
Here Turner represents his seventeenth-century Dutch predecessor Jan van Goyen surveying the harbor of Antwerp in quest
of material.

The portraits on the north wall show Sir Joshua Reynolds
working in two different modes: rather more ceremonious
on the right in his representation of *Elizabeth, Lady Taylor,*
though the landscape detail is relatively unrestrained; rather
more romantic in his depiction on the left of the pensive *Selina,
Lady Skipwith.*

In between hangs *Salisbury Cathedral from the Bishop's Garden*
by John Constable (1776–1837), one of several paintings

48

Riccio, attributed to, *Naked Female Figure*

French, seventeenth century, *Hercules and the Hydra*

depicting the south façade of the building that the artist painted for his friend Dr. John Fisher, Bishop of Salisbury, and the Bishop's family. Another version is in the Metropolitan Museum, New York. The Frick painting, signed and dated 1826, was painted the same year as Turner's *Mortlake Terrace* diagonally across the room.

Another trio of portraits hangs on the window wall: at right, Gainsborough's likeness of *Mrs. Charles Hatchett,* a gifted pianist with whom the painter shared musical interests; at center, the same artist's early, somewhat starched image of *Sarah, Lady Innes;* and at left, Romney's boldly executed portrait of *Miss Mary Finch-Hatton,* painted in 1788.

Sculpture

Along the tops of the bookcases are displayed fifteen small sculptures, all of considerable interest. To the right of the Living Hall door is a bronze lamp representing a *Harpy Bestriding a Grotesque Fish,* one of two versions of this model in The Frick Collection that were executed in Florence during the second half of the sixteenth century. Nearby stands an extraordinary seventeenth-century French bronze of *Hercules and the Hydra* based on a model in the style of Giovanni Bologna. It was cast in approximately twenty separate sections. The hero's head

closely resembles portraits of Henri IV, who was often compared in contemporary literature and engravings to the mythical
Gallic Hercules, and the subjugation of the Hydra apparently
symbolizes Henri's victories over the League. The bronze
Naked Youth with Raised Arms, made probably in Venice in the
early sixteenth century, has been identified at times as a suppliant
and as a Niobid, though a related wooden version shows the
same figure transformed into a St. Sebastian.

Attributed to Severo da Ravenna is the dramatic *Queen
Tomyris with the Head of Cyrus,* depicting the Queen of the
barbarous Massagetae who was responsible for the decapitation
of Cyrus the Great, founder of the Persian Empire and master
of western Asia. A more benign spirit radiates from the terracotta portrait of the Swedish-born miniaturist *Peter Adolf Hall,*
fashioned by Louis-Simon Boizot (1743–1809) around 1775.
The *Naked Female Figure* sometimes attributed to Riccio can be
recognized, with its minute traces of delicate green patination
and its inlaid silver eyes and nipples, as a highly refined simu-
lation of a Hellenistic bronze, and may indeed once have stood
in company with an antique statuette.

The loose-limbed *Hercules in Repose* on the other side of the
fireplace is an important bronze whose maker has not been
satisfactorily identified but who must have been working in
Florence, probably about 1510–15. Some scholars see in this
work a derivation from Michelangelo's lost bronze *David*
completed in 1508.

The sculpture at far right along the north wall portrays
The Grand Dauphin, son of Louis XIV, executed probably in
the eighteenth century after a somewhat larger bronze bust by
François Girardon (1628–1715). The Dauphin's grandson
succeeded Louis XIV in 1715. The existence of so many versions
of *Atlas Supporting the Globe of Heaven* attests to the great
popularity of this combination lamp and inkstand from the
workshop of Andrea Briosco, called Riccio (1460/75?–1532).
Its high quality demonstrates the level on which such decorative
objects could be produced in bulk. Attributed to Riccio himself
is the *Triton and Nereid,* one of the finest examples of another
model highly popular in the early sixteenth century, this one
apparently reflecting the inspiration of Mantegna's engraving
The Battle of the Sea-Gods. At the west end of the wall is a
pendant to *The Grand Dauphin* representing his mother, *Marie-
Thérèse, Queen of France,* executed in the eighteenth century
after a larger marble portrait of about 1700 by Girardon.

The *Hercules* and *Heraldic Wild Man* standing on the bookcase
between the first two windows are identified with the Florentine

Louis-Simon Boizot, *Peter Adolf Hall* (detail)

sculptor Bertoldo di Giovanni (1420/30?–91). The attribution of the latter piece, considered one of the finest surviving early Renaissance bronzes, is supported by resemblances to Bertoldo's bronze *Battle Relief* in Florence. The figure retains extensive traces of its original gilding. The *Hercules* is believed to have been executed by a younger member of Bertoldo's studio.

On the bookcase between the far windows is an elegant statuette of *Paris,* probably once entirely gilt. It seems to be an early sixteenth-century work executed in Nuremberg, with strong reminiscences of the style of Antonio Pollajuolo. The group of *Virtue Overcoming Vice* to its left once formed the lid of an inkstand. As is often the case with small bronzes, it is but one of many versions of the same group, this one believed to have originated in Rome in the late sixteenth century.

On the large table in the center of the room rests an imposing group of a *Triton and Nereid* attributed to Hubert Gerhard (1540/50?–1620). It probably was intended to serve as a fountain, with water emerging from the Triton's mouth and the conch shell. The handsome bronze on the desk at the north end of the room depicts a *Satyr with Inkstand and Candlestick,* yet another example of a decorative sculpture of great quality serving a utilitarian role. It too was produced by Riccio.

Furniture

Most of the furniture in the Library was designed and executed for it. Exceptions are the various side chairs, all in the style of Queen Anne. Four have contemporary needlepoint coverings and two are "scalebacks." The two against the north bookcase are decorated with painted glass crests of the Earls of Scarsdale.

Chinese, Ch'ing dynasty, *Tall Vase with Green Ground*

Giovanni Battista Tiepolo, *Perseus and Andromeda* (detail)

Objects in Gilt Bronze

The neoclassical mantel clock on the central bookcase along the window wall was made in France about 1770, but none of those responsible for its execution have been identified. It is an example of a comparatively rare type of clock fitted with two revolving enameled dials to indicate the minute and the hour. The figures flanking the dials and the reliefs of the Four Seasons that decorate the base all allude to the measurement and passage of time. To either side of the clock are a pair of late Louis XVI candelabra of gilt and patinated bronze representing *Zephyrus* and *Flora*—the subjects of Clodion's neoclassical terracotta group in the Fragonard Room. Made about 1785, the candelabra are notable for the quality of their modeling and chasing.

Porcelains

The Chinese porcelain vases in the Library are all of the type known as *famille noire* or "black hawthorn" enameled ware, with the exception of the rare "green hawthorn" vase in the southeast corner—one of only six known examples of its kind. All date from the Ch'ing dynasty, as do the two small bowls shown against the window wall. The bowl to the right includes representations of dragons unusual for their lack of claws.

53

North Hall

This gallery, which originally overlooked the open carriage court, contains a varied group of works whose common denominator is the color blue.

Paintings

At the south end of the west wall is *The Village of Becquigny* by Pierre-Étienne-Théodore Rousseau (1812–67), one of the artist's most important landscapes. The present luminous blue sky retains only a hint of its earlier sapphire brilliance, which the artist overpainted in response to criticism after the work was shown at the Salon of 1864. Next is the portrait of the *Comtesse d'Haussonville* by Jean-Auguste-Dominique Ingres (1780–1867). The suave fusion of an image of a beautiful and intelligent woman, a minute recording of the paraphernalia of a mid-nineteenth-century Parisian interior, and an elaborate formal design, this composition required many preliminary studies and was executed over a period of at least three years. To the right, *Vétheuil in Winter* by Claude-Oscar Monet (1840–1926) conveys through an unusually limited palette dominated by blues a chilling impression of this small town on the Seine during the severe winter of 1879–80.

Two eighteenth-century masters are represented on the window wall: Giovanni Battista Tiepolo (1696–1770) with *Perseus and Andromeda,* a study for a ceiling fresco in a Milanese palace destroyed by bombing in 1943; and Jean-Baptiste-Siméon Chardin (1699–1779) with his *Lady with a Bird-Organ,* a typically intimate figural composition depicting a woman training a bird to sing. The latter subject was commissioned by Louis XV. Drawings and prints also are displayed occasionally in the North Hall.

Sculpture

The sole sculpture in the North Hall is Houdon's marble bust of *Armand-Thomas Hue, Marquis de Miromesnil,* signed and dated 1777. The subject, who three years earlier had been named *Garde des Sceaux* (Minister of Justice) by Louis XVI, is depicted in the robes and wig of a magistrate. An earlier version of this bust, exhibited in the Salon of 1775, is in the Victoria and Albert Museum, London.

Jean-Auguste-Dominique Ingres, *Comtesse d'Haussonville* (detail)

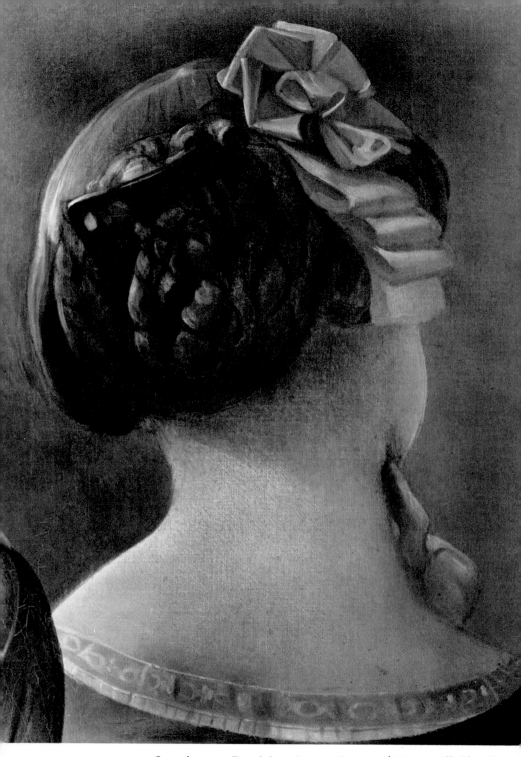

Jean-Auguste-Dominique Ingres, *Comtesse d'Haussonville* (detail)

Furniture

The furniture here includes two armchairs with needlepoint covers belonging to the same set as those in the South Hall and an important blue marble console table commissioned by the Duchesse de Mazarin in 1781 for the grand salon of her house on the Quai Malaquais in Paris. The marble for the table was cut after designs by the architects Jean-François-Thérèse Chalgrin (1739–1811) and François-Joseph Belanger. Pierre Gouthière was responsible for the fine gilt-bronze mounts that balance the mass of the table and give it such a luxurious appearance.

Objects in Gilt Bronze

On the marble table stand a pair of blue Chinese porcelain covered urns of the reign of Ch'ien-lung remodeled about 1770 to fit their neoclassical French mounts of gilt bronze. The motif of the two loving doves on their lids is frequently encountered in late eighteenth-century French decorative art—for example, on the front of Riesener's upright secretary and matching commode in the South Hall.

Gouthière, Chalgrin, and Belanger, *Console Table* (detail)

West Gallery

Sir Anthony Van Dyck,
Margareta Snyders (detail)

The showplace of The Frick Collection and the most museum-like of its interiors is the West Gallery. Though such a gallery now seems an unusual feature in a private residence, similar exhibition spaces were to be found in a number of New York mansions at the turn of the century, including the house Mr. Frick rented prior to building this one. The installation of works of art in the West Gallery is subject to occasional minor changes, but there should be little variation from the locations listed below.

Paintings

As the visitor enters from the North Hall, the first painting on the left is a *Portrait of a Young Artist* long ascribed to Rembrandt but now believed to have been executed by one of the master's pupils.

The brilliant likeness by Sir Anthony Van Dyck (1599–1641) of the painter of animals and still lifes *Frans Snyders* was done probably in Antwerp around 1620. Van Dyck's portrait of his colleague's wife, *Margareta Snyders,* hangs nearby; Mr. Frick apparently took pleasure in reuniting in 1909 this couple whose portraits had been separated since 1793. Between them hangs the largest of the Collection's four paintings by Corot, *The Lake,* painted and exhibited in 1861.

Joseph Mallord William Turner, *The Harbor of Dieppe* (detail)

The West Gallery, shown in a recent view (above) and as
it appeared in the 1920s (left)

Meyndert Hobbema, *Village with Water Mill Among Trees* (detail)

Like a large window, Turner's *The Harbor of Dieppe* seems to open the south wall to let in a flow of golden light. Yet this very brilliance was much criticized when the picture was first shown in 1825. One writer called it "as vicious a specimen as can well be imagined, of mingled truth and falsehood."

The earliest of the four portraits by Frans Hals (1581/85–1666) in the West Gallery is his *Portrait of an Elderly Man*, done about 1627–30. A little farther along hangs the same artist's *Portrait of a Woman* dated 1635. The differences in their painterly execution seem peculiarly appropriate to the characters of the two subjects. Between them is the *Village with Water Mill Among Trees* by Meyndert Hobbema (1638–1709), whose typically centripetal composition draws in the viewer much as does his similar picture in the East Gallery.

The spectacular *White Horse* by Constable was among that artist's earliest successes when exhibited at the Royal Academy in 1819. It remained a favorite picture of the painter, who later called it "one of my happiest efforts on a large scale." Quite a different world is evoked in the nearby portrait by Agnolo Bronzino (1503–72) of *Lodovico Capponi*, painted in Florence about 1550–55. The partially concealed cameo in the subject's right hand is inscribed SORTE (fate or fortune)—a visual

Paolo Veronese, *Allegory of Virtue and Vice*

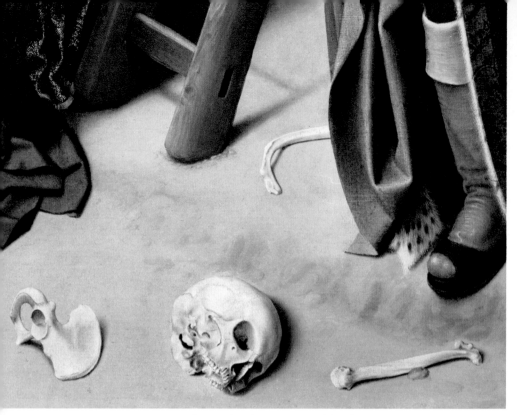

Gerard David, *The Deposition* (detail)

rendering of the idea that fate is obscure.

Towering at the far end of the West Gallery are two canvases by Paolo Caliari, called Il Veronese (c. 1528–88), representing an *Allegory of Virtue and Vice* on the left and an *Allegory of Wisdom and Strength* at right. The former depicts Hercules turning toward Virtue and away from Vice, whose claw-like fingernails have torn at his left leg. The latter suggests the superiority of wisdom over brute force, as well as stating the obvious message of its inscription, OMNIA VANITAS (All is Vanity). Since the two pictures were first recorded in 1621 they have belonged to such prestigious collectors as the Emperor Rudolph II, Queen Christina of Sweden, and the Duc d'Orléans. The archway between the pictures leads to the Enamel Room, which is discussed separately below.

The Deposition by Gerard David (active 1484–1523) is one of the earliest known examples of oil painting on canvas, though it was mounted fairly recently on a mahogany panel.

Rembrandt Harmensz. van Rijn, *The Polish Rider* (detail)

Hals reappears with two portraits painted considerably later than the two across the room. The *Portrait of a Painter,* dating from the early 1650s, has at times been thought to represent Hals himself. The *Portrait of a Man* of about 1660, with its explosive brushwork, is certainly one of the artist's most brilliant late works.

Between these two hangs the haunting *Polish Rider,* painted by Rembrandt Harmensz. van Rijn (1606–69) about 1655. This picture remains an example of how a work of art can elude rational interpretation, for no totally satisfactory explanation of the subject has yet been proposed. It does not seem to be a portrait in the traditional sense, and though all its details are appropriate to the appearance of a Polish cavalry officer, the painting obviously amounts to more than a mere representation of an exotic individual.

After Hals' *Portrait of a Man* hangs *The Education of the Virgin* by Georges de La Tour (1593–1652), depicting the Virgin reading from a Bible held by her mother, St. Anne. While the painting displays the familiar characteristics of La Tour's style, the existence of other versions of the composition suggests that this may possibly be a replica of a work by La Tour executed and signed by his son Étienne.

Turner's *Cologne: The Arrival of a Packet-Boat: Evening* acts as a counterpart to the artist's *Dieppe* directly across the room. Its evening light is appropriately paler and the entire scene much calmer, except for the cluster of excited passengers about to disembark.

Rembrandt's portrait of *Nicolaes Ruts,* signed with a monogram and dated 1631 on the letter the subject holds, may be the artist's first portrait commissioned by someone outside his own family. Its tactile illusionism is characteristic of Rembrandt's early work. The *Landscape with a Footbridge* by Jacob van Ruisdael (1628/29–82) is an unusually hilly subject for a Dutch landscape, and thus probably represents the rolling terrain near the Dutch-German frontier. Heightening its dramatic interest are the various figures, apparently added by another hand—a common practice among landscape painters of the time.

The visitor now encounters a trio of masterpieces. The first is a Rembrandt *Self-Portrait* signed and dated 1658. For all its monumental style and surface richness, this portrait derives its fame ultimately from its simple humanity. Beside it is the last work to be acquired by Mr. Frick, Vermeer's *Mistress and Maid,* believed to have been painted between 1665 and 1670. The nearly blank background may have been left unfinished, as are many of the details. One of the most important works by Diego Velázquez (1599–1660) to be found outside Spain is his portrait of *King Philip IV,* painted in 1644 in the town of Fraga, where Spanish troops, led by Philip in the silver-and-rose costume shown here, had won an important victory over the French.

The portrait of *Vincenzo Anastagi* to the left of the archway leading to the Oval Room was executed by another artist associated with Spain, El Greco, but was painted before he settled there. Anastagi, who probably posed for the picture in Rome sometime between 1571 and 1576, was a distinguished member of the Order of the Knights of Malta. On the right side of the archway is *The Forge* by Francisco de Goya (1746–1828), a scene of contemporary industry derived from traditional representations of Vulcan at his forge but more akin to the realist trends of the nineteenth century than to the mythological themes of the preceding ones.

Francisco de Goya, *The Forge* (detail)

Sculpture

A number of important bronzes are displayed in the West Gallery. Beginning again at the entrance from the North Hall, the nearest object on the table at the east end of the gallery is an *Eve* by Gabriel Grupello (1644–1730), who was born into a noble Milanese family but worked mostly in northern Europe. The work recalls the figure of Eve in Dürer's well-known engraving of *The Fall of Man*. At the center of the table stands a large group of *Nessus and Deianira* attributed to Adriaen de Vries (c. 1560–1626), a variant of a bronze group originally executed by Giovanni Bologna. The splendid, signed statuette of *St. John Baptizing* is the only authenticated small bronze by Francesco da Sangallo (1484–1576) and has been described as the sculptor's masterpiece. It originally stood over the baptismal font in the church of S. Maria delle Carceri at Prato.

On the central table are two tall bronzes—to the east, *Mercury with the Head of Argus,* a Florentine work from the third quarter of the sixteenth century, and to the west, a figure of *Mars* by Tiziano Aspetti (1565–1607). The latter probably once was accompanied by a figure of Venus.

On the table at the west end of the gallery are three remarkable sculptures. *Samson and Two Philistines* is the finest surviving version of several bronzes derived from a lost sketch-model by Michelangelo (1475–1564), who intended to execute the group as a large marble. The smiling *David* in the center of the table was produced probably in Florence in the early sixteenth century and recalls the celebrated *David* of Donatello, as well as that of Verrocchio. The spiraling *Triton Blowing a Trumpet* attributed to Battista Lorenzi (c. 1527–94) may have served as a supporting figure in a table fountain.

Other small sculptures stand on the chests along the walls of the West Gallery. Beneath the large Corot near the North Hall entrance is a *Reliquary Bust of a Female Saint* thought to be the work of the German sculptor Hans Multscher (c. 1400–67). The prominent letter к below the figure's throat indicates that the bust may represent St. Catherine (Katherine) of Alexandria. The *Warrior on Horseback* from the workshop of Riccio farther along the same wall is a popular model that exists in numerous versions.

To the left of the entrance to the Enamel Room is Riccio's splendid *Naked Youth with Raised Left Arm,* an action figure represented in a state of fear. To the right of the arch stands a figure of *Marsyas* executed in the style of Antonio Pollajuolo, creator of the *Hercules* in the Living Hall. Versions of this model are represented in paintings and drawings by Giulio Campagnola, Benozzo Gozzoli, Signorelli, and Uccello, and

Francesco da Sangallo, *St. John Baptizing*

the model may in turn derive from a lost classical prototype.

Beneath Rembrandt's *Polish Rider* is a naturalistic bronze horse, a Paduan work of the early sixteenth century. Like the *Warrior on Horseback* across the gallery and many other statuettes of the period, it recalls the classical horses on the façade of St. Mark's, Venice. Farther along is a *Virgin with the Dead Christ*, a reduced copy, with some variations, of Michelangelo's celebrated marble *Pietà* in St. Peter's, Rome. Many small copies of famous sculptures were produced in the seventeenth century, when this one probably was; it is worth noting that the Frick bronze records the position of the fingers of the Virgin's left hand as they appeared prior to restorations made to the marble in 1736.

Hans Multscher, attributed to, *Reliquary Bust of a Female Saint*

70

At the east end of the gallery are two Italian bronzes representing a *She-Wolf,* both derived from the Etruscan bronze wolf in the Palazzo dei Conservatori, Rome. That below the El Greco dates from the early sixteenth century and may be Paduan. The finer, more naturalistic version beneath the Goya is considered slightly later, but scholars differ over its place of origin. Its rocky base is not bronze, but red marble.

Rugs

The three grand floral rugs in the West Gallery are Persian of the type traditionally called Isfahans but now generally attributed to the looms of Herat. That at the east end is characteristic of a variety introduced in the second half of the sixteenth century. The slightly later rug in the center shows in addition to the usual Herat patterns many cloud bands derived from Chinese sources. Large lanceolate leaves animate the field and border of the rug at the west end of the gallery.

Furniture

Except for the two modern sofas under the Turners, the furniture in the West Gallery consists entirely of walnut pieces dating from the Italian Renaissance and includes examples of three important forms: the large center table, the *cassone* or storage chest, and the folding armchair. Because of their age and the nature of their construction such pieces often include modern replacement elements, but these do not seriously detract from their imposing vigor and beauty.

The only surviving original elements of the table at the east end of the gallery are its two heavy end-supports, with their lion's-paw feet carved in bold relief. The basic form of such tables derives ultimately from Roman marble prototypes that rested on solid end-supports similarly decorated with animal forms.

The massive table at the center of the room, remarkable for its architectural colonnade and its top made of one solid board, appears to be of North Italian origin, perhaps reflecting some French influence. This unique piece bears the arms of the Giovanelli family of Milan and Venice and dates probably from the first half of the sixteenth century.

At the west end of the gallery is a table whose overall form, acanthus decoration, and lion's-paw feet recall, like those of its counterpart at the opposite end of the room, antique examples in marble. Both pieces date from the sixteenth century. This one was formerly in the Davanzati Palace, Florence, and is most likely of Tuscan origin.

The eight *cassoni* along the walls of the West Gallery belong to a type of storage chest that evolved in Italy during the Renaissance, deriving from both antique sarcophagi and Renaissance tombs their overall form and sculptural details. Their deep, polished reliefs, to which gilding often was applied, were intended to approximate the effect of bronzes.

The pair of *cassoni* on the south wall date from the third quarter of the sixteenth century. Lacking identification of the coats of arms they bear, it is difficult to assign them a more precise geographical origin than that suggested by their style—northern Italy. The reliefs on the front of the *cassone* nearer the North Hall entrance depict, on the left, the satyr Marsyas playing a bagpipe before Apollo and two of the Muses and, on the right, Marsyas being flayed by Apollo as a

Italian, sixteenth century, *Cassone* (detail)

river deity observes the grisly fate of a lower being who challenged a god. The subject of Apollo recurs on the matching *cassone*: at left he pursues the nymph Daphne, whose hands are being transformed into the branches of a laurel tree, and at right he plays a viol before a group of animals. *Cassoni* nearly identical to this pair are in the Speed Museum, Louisville, and the Metropolitan Museum, New York. The compositions decorating these pieces seem to be based on contemporary woodcut illustrations for Ovid's *Metamorphoses*.

Flanking the entrance to the Enamel Room are a pair of *cassoni* also from the late sixteenth century, these carved with scenes from the life of Caesar and figures of crouching slaves alongside unidentified coats of arms. The piece at left depicts

Italian, sixteenth century, *Folding Armchair*

73

a triumphal procession headed by Caesar's chariot and including a second chariot full of booty, all reminiscent of Roman sculptural reliefs. The pendant shows Caesar directing the opening of the Roman Treasury and a group of citizens gesturing in amazement before the golden statue of Marius that Caesar had erected during the night.

The *cassoni* with parcel gilding against the north wall are unusual in that both bear the same coat of arms, it being customary to find the husband's arms on one member of a pair and those of the wife on the other. They seem to be of Umbrian or Tuscan origin and to date from the first half of the sixteenth century.

The late sixteenth-century *cassoni* flanking the archway to the Oval Room are decorated with reliefs depicting, on the left, the assassination of Caesar and a triumph of Caesar similar to that on the *cassone* diagonally across the gallery, and, on the right, the slaughter of the sons of Niobe by Apollo and Diana and a scene of homage before an enthroned dignitary.

The eight folding armchairs in the West Gallery are of the type called Savonarola chairs and recall a form of backless seating furniture produced in antiquity. The most interesting are the two with carved coats of arms standing near the center of the south wall.

Andrea del Castagno, attributed to,
The Resurrection (detail)

Enamel Room

Early plans for this oak-paneled room, so dramatically different in scale and atmosphere from the adjoining West Gallery, identified it merely as "Mr. Frick's Room," but on subsequent drawings it is labeled "The Limoges Gallery," in reference to the important collection of French painted enamels Mr. Frick began acquiring in 1915 and for which the interior was modified. The installation of the enamels in tiers recalls the Renaissance manner of massing these precious objects.

Gentile da Fabriano, *Madonna and Child, with Saints Lawrence and Julian* (detail)

Paintings

Nine Renaissance paintings from Italy and northern Europe are displayed here. To the left of the entrance hangs *The Resurrection,* a work in tempera generally attributed to Andrea del Castagno (before 1420–1457) or his shop. It and several related panels probably once were subsidiary elements in a large polyptych.

The small but brilliantly colored altarpiece alongside was painted in the early 1420s in Tuscany by Gentile da Fabriano (c. 1370–1427), whose signature is visible on the frame. The kneeling figures adoring the Virgin and Child represent St. Lawrence at left and St. Julian at right.

The product of a more worldly attitude than Gentile's ecstatic devotional image is the *Portrait of a Man* by Hans Memling (c. 1440–94), one of the most successful portraitists of his time. The Frick panel may be Memling's earliest known portrait with a landscape background.

Across the room is a fragment of one of the most celebrated painted works of the early Renaissance—the *Maestà,* a huge altarpiece executed in 1308–11 by Duccio di Buoninsegna (c. 1255–1319) for the main altar of the Duomo in Siena. The Frick panel, *The Temptation of Christ on the Mountain,* is one of several small scenes that were detached from the altarpiece and are now widely scattered. Christ is shown rejecting Satan, who tempts him with the kingdoms of the world.

The tall panel thought to represent *St. Simon the Apostle* is another detached element from an altarpiece, in this case one of four wing panels of a polyptych painted by Piero della Francesca (1410/20–92) for the main altar of the church of S. Agostino in the artist's Tuscan home town of Borgo Sansepolcro. The altarpiece was commissioned in 1454 and apparently completed by 1469. The other wing panels are in Lisbon, London, and Milan.

The powerful *Pietà with Donor* was acquired by Mr. Frick as a work of Antonello da Messina, but it is now generally believed to have been painted in southeastern France by an unknown artist. It is a copy with variations of a *Pietà* without a donor attributed to a follower of the Swiss painter Konrad Witz. Dates proposed for the execution of the *Pietà with Donor* range from 1440 to 1480.

Across the room, another kneeling donor appears in the small panel of *Christ Bearing the Cross, with a Dominican Friar,* by the master traditionally known as Barna da Siena (active around 1350). The figure of Christ seen here closely resembles the one found in the fresco depicting the *Way to Calvary* that Barna painted for the Collegiata at San Gimignano.

Piero della Francesca, *St. Simon the Apostle (?)*

Duccio di Buoninsegna, *The Temptation of Christ on the Mountain* (detail)

Jan van Eyck, *Virgin and Child, with Saints and Donor* (detail)

Alongside this panel hangs one of the very few paintings in American museums by Jan van Eyck (active 1422–41), his *Virgin and Child, with Saints and Donor,* presumed to have been begun by the artist during his last years but completed after his death by an assistant, perhaps Petrus Christus (d. 1472/73). St. Barbara is shown at left behind the donor, Jan Vos, in white Carthusian habit, and at right stands St. Elizabeth of Hungary. Beyond St. Elizabeth's head appears a large church that many believe represents old St. Paul's in London, which van Eyck could have seen and drawn during his diplomatic visit to England in 1428–29.

The little panel of *The Three Soldiers* is a rare grisaille signed by Pieter Bruegel the Elder (active 1551–69) and dated 1568. It was once in the collection of Charles I of England, to whom it was given by the poet Endymion Porter. Represented are three German *Landsknechte,* or mercenary soldiers—a standard-bearer, a drummer, and a fifer.

Jean de Court, *Plaque: The Adoration of the Shepherds* (detail)

Sculpture

All the sculptures in the Enamel Room are bronze works dating from the Italian Renaissance. Following the same order as that taken with the paintings, the first object is a richly ornamented *Hand Bell* ascribed to the Paduan sculptor Gian Girolamo Grandi (1508–60). The bell is ornamented with a motif related to the impresa of Bernard Cles, Bishop of Trent, who also employed Grandi for several other commissions. The motif of the putto sitting on—or more normally leaning against—a skull was a common theme in Renaissance art.

The graceful *Faun Playing the Flute* by the Venetian sculptor Vettor Gambello, called Camelio (c. 1455/60–1537), is a fine version of a model known in a number of examples. Originally the figure held a double flute. Its intricate pose is derived from a Roman sarcophagus relief.

Riccio's *Lamp* in the form of a shoe richly ornamented with minute reliefs of classical motifs is considered one of the sculptor's masterpieces. It was recorded and reproduced in

Gian Girolamo Grandi, *Hand Bell*

engravings as early as 1652, when it was in a Paduan collection.

Across the room, beneath Piero della Francesca's *St. Simon,* is a small *David,* one of many such figures executed in the studio of Bartolomeo Bellano (c. 1434–96/97) or possibly in another Paduan workshop after Bellano's death. The figure recalls the bronze *David* of Donatello, with whom Bellano appears to have been associated in Florence.

Beneath van Eyck's *Virgin and Child* are a pair of Paduan or Venetian *Candlesticks* from the second quarter of the sixteenth century flanking a *Casket* based on a model by Severo da Ravenna. The arms on the lid of the *Casket* are those of the Roman house of Cesi. Over twenty similar boxes are known.

Riccio, *Lamp*

Furniture

Several pieces from The Frick Collection's small but rich holdings of French Renaissance furniture are exhibited in the Enamel Room, all of them executed in walnut. To the right as the visitor enters is a table from the late sixteenth century remarkable for the quality of its carved ornament, notably the animal masks on the base and the corner columns decorated with spiraling leafy vines. The table from the same period to the left of the entrance has end-supports carved with elegantly proportioned male and female figures.

The two trapezoidal armchairs against the window wall are of a sixteenth-century type sometimes called *caquetoire*. Their form may derive from a chair without arms produced earlier in Italy and called a *sgabello*. The chair on the left is carved with an illusionistic relief depicting an archway. Much of its construction is recent. The chair to the right, for the most part in its original condition, has a particularly rich back and cresting carved in high relief.

French, sixteenth century, *Armchair*

Enamels
The group of painted enamels displayed here has been described as one of the finest selections of this craft in the United States. The pieces were all executed at Limoges in central France between the early sixteenth and the mid-seventeenth centuries by members of artisan families who sustained their guild privileges from one generation to the next. Originally the enamelers, who were also goldsmiths, relied on pattern books for their images, but during the sixteenth century they turned to individual engraved scenes for sources, copying subjects directly from prints by Northern, Italian, and French artists. Following medieval tradition, their subjects and forms were at first religious—as seen here in the devotional plaques and triptychs—but starting around 1530 their production expanded

Master of the Passion, attributed to, *Plaque:*
The Seven Sorrows of the Virgin

to include portraits and articles of luxury ware, such as caskets, saltcellars, bowls, dishes, candlesticks, and ewers. The splendor of these intricately crafted objects, as well as their jewel-like coloring, unaltered by time, made them highly sought after by collectors. Most of the enamels in The Frick Collection were acquired by Mr. Frick from the estate of J. Pierpont Morgan.

Included among the works in the north case, to the right as the visitor enters, are seven triptychs and four plaques that demonstrate the origins of Limoges painted enamels in the religious art of the Middle Ages. The earliest and perhaps rarest is the triptych at lower left by the Master of the Baltimore and Orléans Triptychs (late fifteenth–early sixteenth centuries). The unusual double triptych by Nardon Pénicaud (c. 1470–1541) at the center of the top shelf is one of the most sumptuous pieces in the group, while the anonymous *Seven Sorrows of the Virgin* at lower right is among the more subtle and mysterious. Nardon's brother Jean I Pénicaud (c. 1480–after 1541) is represented by four imposing works. Across the central tier are outstanding examples of household objects transformed into *objets d'art* by artisans such as Pierre Reymond (c. 1513–after 1584), Couly II Noylier (active 1539–after 1571), and Suzanne Court (late sixteenth–early seventeenth centuries).

The enamels in the south case are primarily secular. At the top are two oval dishes and a ewer stand by Jean (d. 1602/03), Pierre, and Martial Reymond (d. 1599); the composition of *Moses Striking the Rock* is based on woodcut illustrations by Bernard Salomon, that of *Apollo and the Muses* on an engraving by Giorgio Ghisi after a drawing by Luca Penni. Seven portrait plaques by the illustrious Léonard Limousin (c. 1505–75/77) represent notable figures of sixteenth-century France, among them Guy Chabot, Baron de Jarnac, and his wife; Odet de Coligny, Cardinal de Châtillon; and, in an extraordinary allegorical composition, five members of the powerful House of Guise. The most spectacular of the Collection's pieces is the large plaque at right of *The Adoration of the Shepherds,* adapted from Bronzino's celebrated painting. It was enameled by Jean de Court (active c. 1555–85), who was also responsible for the ewer and two footed bowls in this case. Pierre Courteys (c. 1520–before 1591) is represented by two large caskets, and Jean Guibert (late sixteenth–early seventeenth centuries), whose signature was recently identified for the first time, produced the two richly ornamented saltcellars.

Workshop of Pierre Reymond,
Saltcellar in Baluster Form: Amorini and Satyrs

Pierre Reymond, *Casket: Old Testament Subjects*

Pottery

Contemporary with the Limoges enamels and reminiscent of them in form is the rare earthenware *Ewer* in the south case, attributed to the sixteenth-century workshops of Saint-Porchaire in west-central France. Characteristic of this precious pottery are the marbleized handle, the three-dimensional applied ornaments including chimeras and salamanders, and the intricately patterned surface decoration.

Saint-Porchaire Pottery, *Ewer*

Oval Room   The Oval Room, at the far end of the West Gallery opposite the Enamel Room, was created in 1931–35, replacing Mr. Frick's office and the north exit from the original open carriage court. In form the room recalls projects for a two-story gallery that Mr. Frick was at the time of his death considering building to house his sculpture collection.

James Abbott McNeill Whistler, *Valerie, Lady Meux* (detail)

James Abbott McNeill Whistler, *Robert,*
Comte de Montesquiou-Fezensac (detail)

Paintings

The four pictures in the Oval Room are by the only American painter other than Stuart and Johansen who is represented in the Collection: James Abbott McNeill Whistler (1834–1903). All are portraits, and all originally bore abstract or musical titles of the type the artist frequently employed.

On the left as the visitor enters from the West Gallery is a portrait of *Valerie, Lady Meux,* originally entitled *Harmony in Pink and Gray.* Lady Meux was the first to give Whistler a commission after his bankruptcy, and in all he painted her three times. Rising from humble origins, she married the brewer Henry Bruce Meux. Her colorful personality is suggested by the appearance she once made at a hunt riding an elephant.

Mrs. Frederick R. Leyland is represented wearing a dress designed by Whistler himself. The pale, restricted palette led the artist to entitle this work *Symphony in Flesh Colour and Pink* when it was first exhibited in 1874. The subject's husband was one of Whistler's chief patrons and commissioned him to paint the famous Peacock Room now in the Freer Gallery, Washington.

Across the Oval Room hangs Whistler's austere portrait of the French poet and socialite *Robert, Comte de Montesquiou-Fezensac,* who is considered one of the sources for the character of Baron de Charlus in Proust's *Remembrance of Things Past.* Begun in London in 1891, the portrait was completed in Paris the following year and was shown to acclaim—and ridicule—at the Paris International Exposition of 1894. Like its companions, it was once exhibited with a typically Whistlerian title, *Arrangement in Black and Gold.* The only trace of gold now visible is in the signature.

The portrait of *Miss Rosa Corder,* originally called *Arrangement in Black and Brown,* depicts a fellow artist who caught Whistler's eye one day as she passed before a black door wearing a brown dress. The many prolonged sittings Whistler required for it lasted on occasion until his subject fainted. The passage of time and Whistler's dubious working procedures and materials have left this portrait and that of Montesquiou perhaps less legible than the artist intended.

Sculpture

Houdon's *Diana the Huntress* has been described as "an example of technical virtuosity that surpasses anything else achieved by Houdon in this material, or by any sculptor before him." It is made of at least ten sections, separately fired and then joined and fitted with supporting metal armatures. Its present painted surface, which conceals the junctions, dates from extensive restorations carried out in 1910–11, but the figure had been painted originally. The sculpture, one of only five life-size terracottas created by Houdon, is probably the *"Diane"* recorded in the Houdon sale catalogue of 1795. A marble version, with plant forms supporting the figure, once belonged to Catherine II and is now in the Gulbenkian Foundation, Lisbon; a plaster and two bronze versions from Houdon's workshop exist as well.

Furniture

The eight English side chairs are in the Queen Anne style. Their walnut frames are upholstered in composite needlepoint coverings, with the older petit point sections dating from around the first quarter of the eighteenth century.

European, c. 1690–1725, *Needlepoint Chair Covering* (detail)

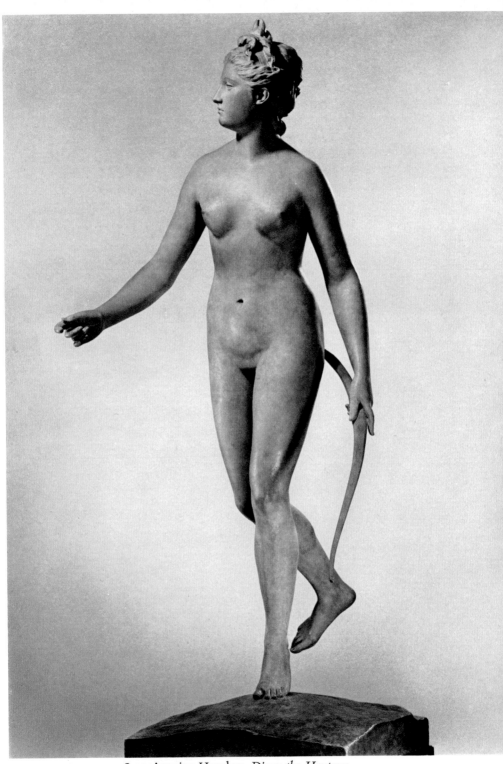

Jean-Antoine Houdon, *Diana the Huntress*

Aelbert Cuyp, *Dordrecht: Sunrise* (detail)

East Gallery

The East Gallery, like the Oval Room, was added to the Collection's original building in 1931–35, and was remodeled in 1963–64 to have it more closely resemble the other exhibition spaces. It contains a characteristically eclectic group of pictures and objects.

Hilaire-Germain-Edgar Degas, *The Rehearsal* (detail)

El Greco, *The Purification of the Temple* (detail)

Paintings

To the left as one enters from the Oval Room hangs a portrait of *The Hon. Frances Duncombe* by Gainsborough. Comparison with the large portrait of *Paola Adorno* by Van Dyck across the room reveals how much the British artist owed his seventeenth-century Flemish predecessor in terms of the scale of the composition, the proportions of the figure, and even the style of the costume.

The *Quay at Amsterdam* by Jacob van Ruisdael is a rare urban scene by an artist better known for his landscapes, such as the one in the West Gallery. The painting depicts the Dam, the main square of Amsterdam near the present railroad station, and beyond it the body of water known as the Damrak, now filled in.

Hobbema's *Village Among Trees* is almost the twin of the same artist's landscape in the West Gallery, but this picture was painted on oak panel rather than on canvas and it bears a date—1665. Though Hobbema's work is repetitive, it maintains a certain freshness and a high level of technical virtuosity.

Goya's intense, romantic portrait of a Spanish officer tentatively identified as the *Conde de Tepa* was acquired by Mr. Frick from the collection of José Lázaro Galdeano in Madrid in 1914.

Van Dyck's large portrait of *James, Seventh Earl of Derby, His Lady and Child* is a grand composition representative of the artist's last English period, 1632–41. The Earl was a constitutional Royalist who fought in the army of Charles II. He was captured and executed in 1651. His wife, the eldest daughter of the Duc de Thouars, valiantly defended the Derbys' country seat during his absence in 1644. The identity of their young daughter is uncertain; the color of her dress may refer to her descent on her mother's side from the House of Orange.

The second of the three portraits by Goya in the East Gallery is believed to represent *Doña María Martínez de Puga,* who has been described as Goya's landlady in Bordeaux or his landlady's daughter. In the year this portrait is dated—1824—the artist left Madrid and settled in Bordeaux, where he died four years later.

Like Goya, Aelbert Cuyp (1620–91) is also represented by three pictures in the East Gallery. The first, *Dordrecht: Sunrise,* is the sort of Dutch landscape that Turner echoed in such works as his *Cologne* in the West Gallery; in turn, Cuyp in this work of about 1650 may well have been influenced by the light-filled canvases of his French contemporary Claude Lorrain. For all its impressionistic magic, the picture delineates with topographical precision the port city of Dordrecht and its outskirts. On a much smaller scale, Cuyp represents in the adjacent *River Scene* several small passenger boats sailing along an inland Dutch waterway under a luminous, dramatic sky.

In contrast to the dry brushwork and nearly monochromatic harmonies of Goya's *Puga* portrait, that of *Don Pedro, Duque de Osuna,* the first painting on the east wall, has the lush manner and silvery tones of Goya's earlier years, though this engaging work may have been painted as late as 1795. The Duke was one of Spain's leading noblemen and among Goya's principal patrons.

The sole painting of its genre in The Frick Collection, the *Still Life with Plums* by Chardin is a characteristically simple-seeming work by this artist whose "magic" realism was praised by Diderot and whose compositions were freshly appreciated by the Cubists in the early years of the twentieth century. The canvas appears to date from about 1730.

The Sermon on the Mount by Claude Lorrain (1600–82) is one of the artist's most ambitious and complex works, yet it maintains the natural harmony and poetic luminosity associated with the artist's name. Painted in 1656 for François Bosquet, Bishop of Montpellier, the picture was later in the collection of William Beckford at Fonthill Abbey (where it narrowly escaped destruction by fire) and belonged to the Duke of Westminster before The Frick Collection acquired it in 1960.

El Greco treated the theme of *The Purification of the Temple* frequently, both in Italy and after he settled in Spain. At his death four paintings of the subject, possibly including this one, were among his effects, and at least five autograph versions of the composition are known today. The Frick painting has a special emotional intensity that is all the greater for its small size.

An antecedent for the nineteenth-century pastoral subjects Mr. Frick admired in the early years of his collecting is found in Cuyp's *Cows and Herdsman by a River*. The ruined castle on the far bank may be the Huis te Merwede outside Dordrecht, the city Cuyp represented in the large riverscape on the north wall.

The sympathetic portrait of the *Comtesse Daru* by Jacques-Louis David (1748–1825) suggests the subject's personality as it was described by her admirer, Stendhal: "Her appearance reveals a warm temperament.... Her features reveal a forceful, frank, and jolly character." The Countess' husband, who was master of Napoleon's household, secured for David the long-awaited payment for his painting of the coronation of Napoleon and Josephine, and it was to thank him that David secretly painted this portrait, signing it at four o'clock on March 14, 1810.

Dominating the south wall is Van Dyck's majestic portrait of *Paola Adorno, Marchesa di Brignole Sale,* member of a distinguished Genoese family who married Anton Giulio Brignole, a writer and civic leader. Another portrait of her by Van Dyck hangs in the former Brignole residence in Genoa, the Palazzo Rosso, and one depicting her with her son is in the National Gallery, Washington. The Frick portrait was executed between 1622 and 1627.

The Rehearsal, a classic treatment of a ballet subject by Edgar Degas (1834–1917), was probably shown by the artist in the fourth exhibition of the Impressionists in 1879. Among the many studies Degas made for this seemingly casual composition is a drawing of the aged violinist, now in the Minneapolis Institute of Arts.

Jean-Baptiste Greuze, *The Wool Winder* (detail)

The Wool Winder by Jean-Baptiste Greuze (1725–1805) is
a fine example of that artist's early manner, influenced by
Chardin's work but lighter in both spirit and execution.
The letter B on the chair rail suggests that this may be a portrait of a member of the Babuti family, into which Greuze
had married the year he exhibited this painting at the
Academy—1759.

Gainsborough's full-length portrait of *Mrs. Peter William
Baker,* dated 1781, depicts his subject standing in romantic
isolation under rather threatening skies—a type of setting he
occasionally used as background for images of forlorn country
waifs. The portrait hung at the Bakers' country seat in Dorset-
shire until Mr. Frick acquired it in 1917.

Sculpture

The characteristically complex *Satyr with Inkstand and Candle-stick* under the Van Dyck *Derby* group is considered an autograph bronze by Riccio. The arms on the inkstand are those of the Capodivacca family of Padua.

Though features of the bronze group of a *Satyr Mother with a Child Satyr* across the room recall the work of Riccio, the naturalistic treatment of the base suggests that the piece was executed in a northern European center such as Nuremberg in the last quarter of the sixteenth century. It was probably intended to serve as a saltcellar.

Furniture

The French Renaissance table in the center of the room combines late Gothic elements, such as the draw-top, with motifs revived from antiquity, as seen in the richly carved sculptural ornaments. The piece dates from the second half of the sixteenth century.

The two chests of drawers in the East Gallery bear the stamp of Carel, an *ébéniste* about whom little is known except that he was active in Paris from the mid-1730s to the mid-1750s. With their elaborate end-cut *(bois de bout)* floral marquetry and scrolling gilt-bronze mounts, the two commodes give the appearance of being identical. However, there are differences in their marquetry patterns and in the construction of their sides, which in the case of the chest against the north wall, acquired fifty years after the other to form a pair, are more *bombé*.

The eight armchairs, whose frames are modern, form two groups. The pair against the west wall are covered in Gobelins tapestries woven about 1755–70 after designs by Boucher from a series known as *Les Enfants jardiniers*. The other six bear tapestries woven at an unidentified French manufactory in the nineteenth century, with the seat coverings probably based on eighteenth-century cartoons.

The rug is modern.

Gobelins Manufactory, after François Boucher,
Tapestry Chair Covering

Jacques Jonghelinck, *The Duke of Alba* (detail)

Antoine Coysevox, *Robert de Cotte*

Federico Brandani, *Antonio Galli* (detail)

Garden Court Leaving the East Gallery through the southwest door, the visitor passes through a small vestibule that gives access to the Lecture Room and then enters the Garden Court, designed by John Russell Pope to replace the open carriage court of the original Frick residence. The Court's paired Ionic columns and symmetrical planting beds were to be echoed in the same architect's design for the original building of the National Gallery in Washington. In addition to providing a respite for visitors with its plants and fountain, the room also houses an imposing group of bronze sculptures.

Sculpture To the right as one enters is the grand bust of *Henri de La Tour d'Auvergne, Maréchal Turenne,* one of France's greatest military leaders of the seventeenth century. This may well be the bust of Turenne that Antoine Coysevox (1640–1720) exhibited at the Salon of 1704. In 1800, by order of Napoleon, Turenne's remains were reinterred along with those of other military giants in the church of Les Invalides.

In the northwest corner of the court is a *Bust of a Jurist,* probably a professor at the University of Padua, attributed to Danese Cattaneo (c. 1509–73). The almost illegible inscription implausibly identifying the subject as Titian seems much later than the mid-sixteenth-century piece itself and is not to be credited.

At the southwest end of the court is a bust of the humanist, diplomat, and poet *Antonio Galli* by Federico Brandani (c. 1522/25–75), a sculptor who worked primarily in Urbino. In the central niche to the left is Coysevox's bust of *Robert de Cotte,* probably the most influential French architect of his time; this piece was executed in the early years of the eighteenth century.

On the far side of the portal leading back to the Entrance Hall is an austere bust of the *Duke of Alba* by the Flemish sculptor Jacques Jonghelinck (1530–1606). Don Fernando, third Duke of Alba, served as Spanish Viceroy and Captain General in the Netherlands, where he established a reputation for ruthless repression of heresy and nationalism. This bust, dated 1571, is related to a full-length portrait of him that Jonghelinck executed the same year, casting it from captured cannon.

In the circular recesses that interrupt the cornice at the north and south ends of the court have been placed a *Head of a Boy* possibly representing Mars and a *Head of a Girl* thought to represent Venus, both French works of the eighteenth century.

The most remarkable sculpture in the Garden Court stands

near the fountain—a bronze *Angel* whose date of completion is precisely inscribed on the inside of the left wing: March 28, 1475. The inscription also records that the work was cast by Jean Barbet of Lyon, a founder of cannon who was probably casting a work designed by someone else. The history of this figure is uncertain. It most likely adorned the exterior of a building, perhaps even the Sainte-Chapelle in Paris, which was partially reconstructed in 1460.

In the farther niches at either side of the passage leading back to the Entrance Hall are a pair of bronze *Female Figures with Cornucopias*. Originally intended to serve as candelabra, they probably were produced in a Venetian workshop around the middle of the sixteenth century.

Jean Barbet, *Angel* (detail at left)

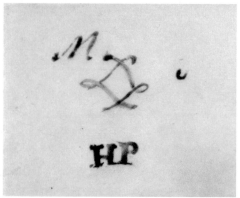

Jean-Louis Morin and Henri-Martin
Prévost, Sèvres Manufactory, *Water Jug*

François Boucher,
The Four Seasons: Autumn

Jean-Baptiste-Camille Corot,
The Boatman of Mortefontaine

Clodion, *Zephyrus and Flora*

Vecchietta, *The Resurrection*

François-Hubert Drouais, *The Comte and
Chevalier de Choiseul as Savoyards*

Francisco de Goya, *Don Pedro,*
Duque de Osuna

Jean-Antoine Houdon, *Armand-Thomas*
Hue, Marquis de Miromesnil

Chinese, Ch'ing dynasty,
Tall Vase with Black Ground

Jacques-Louis David, *Comtesse Daru*

Giovanni Bellini, *St. Francis in Ecstasy*

Carel, *Commode*

Index

Staircase, The Frick Collection

François Boucher, *Madame Boucher*

Jean-Henri Riesener, *Secretary*

Sèvres Manufactory, *Pot-Pourri Myrte*

Fragonard Room, The Frick Collection

Living Hall, The Frick Collection

Michelangelo Buonarroti, after, *Samson and Two Philistines*

Martial Reymond, *Concave Oval Plaque: Ceres Holding a Torch*

Garden Court, The Frick Collection